# THE FLIP LIFE

# THE FLIP LIFE

**If you can't change your view, change your view.**

**AMIT DHAWAN**

NU VOICE
PRESS

First published by NU VOICE PRESS 2025
An imprint of Hubhawks Pvt. Ltd
www.nuvoicepress.com



The characters and events portrayed in this book are fictitious. Any similarity to real persons, living or dead, is coincidental and not intended by the author.



ISBN: 978-81-990481-6-4

Printed at
Published by: Nu Voice Press

# CONTENTS

Truth doesn't always soothe. Sometimes, it stings first. When clarity arrives, it often brings decisions, not peace.

# PREFACE

It didn't take me months to write this book.
It took 32 years.
Because it's not just filled with words.
It's filled with lived moments, quiet reflections, small breakdowns,
and those rare breakthroughs when the world didn't change,
but something inside did.
*The Flip Life* is not a guide.
It won't give you 5 hacks to success.
It won't tell you to wake up at 5 a.m., hustle harder,
or manifest your way into a mansion.
These aren't just my lessons.
They're borrowed from what I've lived,
what I've witnessed,
what I've overheard in late-night conversations and silent observations.
From the stories people don't tell out loud,
but show you if you pay attention.
You don't have to read this book cover to cover.
Just flip to any page,
and let it flip something in you.
*The Flip Life* is not about having all the answers.
It's about shifting the question.
It's about realizing that clarity isn't always loud.
And perspective is everything.
I didn't write this as a guru.
I wrote it as a mirror.
For anyone who's ever paused in the middle of the mess and thought:
*"There's got to be another way of seeing this."*
This book is that other way.
Welcome to *The Flip Life.*
Make it yours.

*"I wrote this to remind myself too."*
—Amit

# CHAPTER I

# PERSPECTIVE IS EVERYTHING

*Life will turn upside down if you just change the way you look at it.*

It's the same room.
The same job.
The same face in the mirror.
But the energy changes when your lens gets clearer.

You thought it was failure, but it was redirection.
You called it rejection, but it was protection.
That delay that drained you? A blessing in disguise.
That heartbreak you feared? What helped you rise.

Most of what hurts isn't what's real.
It's how we frame what we feel.

You can call it chaos, or you can call it shift.
You can say you're stuck, or see the gift.
You can drown in "Why me?"
Or rise with "What now?"
You can hold the pain,
Or break the vow:
That every setback must steal your spark,
That every ending must leave you in the dark.

Because life is waiting to rearrange
The moment you choose to see it strange.
To tilt your head. To flip the script.
To question the weight of what you've gripped.

You don't need the world to change a bit.
Just change the way you look at it!

***Right or wrong is just a perspective. What is right for you is wrong for someone else.***

You call it wrong,
They call it life.
You call it truth,
They call it strife.

You see a problem,
They see a path.
You choose stillness,
They choose wrath.

Right and wrong aren't written in air-tight code.
They shift with the weight of the road you've rode.

You may see eating meat as cruel, unjust.
They may see it as nature, survival, trust.
One calls it violence. One calls it tradition.
Both hold truth in their own definition.

The world isn't built in black and white.
It's lived in shades of shadow and light.

What you label selfish, someone calls sane.
What you think is healing, they call pain.

Even love. Even faith. Even peace. Even war.
All look different from someone else's shore.

So, before you dismiss or call someone blind,
Ask what shaped their heart, ask what built their mind.

You don't have to bend. You don't have to agree.
But remember, to understand is to be free.

Because the truth is this, and it always compels:
What feels right to you, might feel wrong to someone else.

***When you look at them from your eyes, you're judging them. When you look at the world from theirs, you're understanding them.***

You see them act.
You hear their tone.
You build a story from what's shown.

"She's rude."
"He's cold."
"They're selfish."
"They fold."

But what if that silence was learned, not chosen?
What if their strength is how they stay frozen?
What if that anger is shielding grief,
And the loudest one in the room needs relief?

It's easy to label from where you stand.
Harder to see with a different hand.
We judge the mask, ignore the scar.
We forget how different our journeys are.

Maybe they weren't taught how to explain.
Maybe they've only known life through pain.
Maybe what looks like distance or pride
Is just someone protecting what's hurting inside.

You don't have to agree.
But you can try to see.
You don't need to carry their weight as your own,
But you can stop throwing the first stone.

Compassion begins where certainty ends.
And most strangers are softer than they pretend.

So before you decide who they've become,
Pause your lens, and shift the outcome.

Because when you look at them from your eyes, you're judging them.
When you look at the world from theirs, you're understanding them.

***You can either crib about the cards you're dealt, or focus on how you want to play with them.***

Some are born with a head start.
Some begin at the back of the line.
Some get love with no effort.
Some spend years begging for a sign.

Some are handed comfort.
Others learn to fight.
Some walk in daylight.
Some crawl through night.

Life doesn't always deal fair or clean.
It gives some gold, while others stay unseen.

But the game isn't won in the opening hand.
It's in how you move, where you choose to stand.
You can keep counting all that went wrong,
Or start building your own kind of strong.

You can stay bitter,
Or get better.
Hold the weight,
Or make it lighter.

You don't control the cards that fall.
But you do decide if you rise at all.

So ask yourself when the odds feel grim,
Do you want to lose, or learn to swim?

Because life won't always play like a gem.
You can either crib about the cards you're dealt,
Or focus on how you want to play with them.

***What's important: winning, or playing to win?***

Everyone wants the trophy.
The stage.
The light.
The applause that says, "You got it right."

But few want the early mornings.
The silent grind.
The days with no feedback,
No finish line.

It's easy to crave the high of the end.
Harder to show up when there's nothing to defend.

Because winning is loud,
But growth is slow.
And most of the magic is in what no one will know.

It's in showing up when you feel unseen,
In failing once, twice, seventeen.
It's in choosing to try when doubt is loud,
In building alone, without the crowd.

True success is not a single spin.
It's how you train your heart to play for the win.

When you chase only titles, you burn out fast.
But when you chase the process, the joy will last.

So the real question isn't what you've already done.
It's how you play when you haven't yet won.

Because medals fade and applause grows thin.
What matters is playing like you're in it to win.

***Every problem has a solution. If it doesn't, it's not a problem. It's a situation. Situations require acceptance.***

You spill a drink, you clean it up.
You lose a file, you back it up.
You miss a turn, you take the next.
You solve the puzzle. You fix the text.

That's a problem; it comes, it goes.
With effort, thought, or someone who knows.

But what about things that won't shift with speed?
Like timing that's wrong, or a person in need.
Like wanting a yes where there's only a no.
Or asking for more when it's time to let go.

You try to explain it, fix it, reframe it.
But nothing moves, no matter how you name it.

And that's when you learn there's a different game.
It's not about solving or assigning blame.
It's about seeing that some things just stay.
And your peace comes from getting out of the way.

It's not giving up,
It's giving in,
To the kind of wisdom that comes from within.

So ask yourself the next time you're seeking a sign,
Is this a problem? Or just life's design?

Because some things don't move, no matter the tension.
And those aren't problems.
They're situations that need your acceptance.

***Opinions are always biased. Listen to yourself.***

They'll tell you to wait.
They'll tell you to run.
They'll say what's risky,
And what looks fun.

They'll speak from love.
They'll speak from fear.
Some advice will calm you.
Some won't feel clear.

Even when they mean the best,
Their words are shaped by their own test,
By what they've lost,
By what they've missed,
By chances taken or dismissed.

So while they speak with care and grace,
Remember, they don't stand in your place.
Their path was theirs, with their own rules,
And what served them might not serve you.

You're allowed to nod, and still decline,
To hear their thoughts, but draw your line.
Take the parts that truly land.
Leave the rest, and understand.

You know the rhythm of your flame.
You carry your own map and name.
And though their words may help a bit,
Only your heart knows what truly fits.

So thank them all, and take only what fits your shelf.
Opinions are always biased. Listen to yourself.

***While you try to find the "next big thing," don't miss out on the current.***

You're chasing more.
A bigger stage.
A better title.
The next page.
A job that pays.
A love that stays.
A sign that says,
"You've made it, praise."

You're building futures in your head,
But missing what today just said.

The tea that's warm.
The sky that's clear.
The friend who checks in year after year.
The small win buried in routine.
The peace that hides in between.

We're told to dream.
To scale. To grow.
To never settle. To stay in flow.

But sometimes growth is not a race.
It's noticing what already fills the space.
It's looking around, not always ahead.
It's feeling full instead of fed.

The moment you're in is not a draft.
It won't replay. It won't come back.

So dream big dreams, but don't forget,
Life's best parts often come unmeant.

The future matters, but here's the hint:
While you try to find the next big thing,
Don't miss out on the current.

***The amount of mind space you free up just by being honest all the time is unbelievable.***

Lying takes work.
Even the small kind.
You have to keep track.
You fall behind.

What you told them.
What you told her.
What you left out.
What you had to blur.

It piles up,
Version after version.
A full-time job,
Of quiet diversion.

But honesty?
That's freedom in plain clothes.
No timelines to manage.
No tangled flows.

You speak once, that's it.
No edits. No spin.
What you said at the start
Still holds at the end.

You don't second-guess.
You don't rewind.
You sleep better
Because your story aligns.

It's not just about truth, it's about being clear.
No more pretending. No more fear.

Because when your words match what's real and believable,
The space in your mind becomes unbelievable.

***You can either keep cribbing or call it learning and move on.***

You tried your best,
It didn't land.
You gave your all,
Life changed the plan.

You trusted someone,
They let you down.
You dreamed aloud,
The world just frowned.

And now you stand at a simple choice:
Hold the hurt, or change the voice.

You can replay the pain.
You can list what went wrong.
You can stay in the story
For way too long.

Or you can zoom out.
Take the hit with grace.
Ask what it taught you,
And shift your pace.

Because cribbing keeps you stuck in the scene.
Learning clears the space in between.

Every mistake holds a map inside.
Every detour teaches where not to hide.

You don't have to love what the past became,
But you can choose not to hold it the same.

It happened. It stung. The damage is done.
What matters now is where you run.

Let go of the loop you've been leaning on.
You can either keep cribbing, or call it learning and move on.

*You don't get independence by asking for it. You have to claim it.*

Independence isn't granted.
It's not gifted by a nod.
It's not waiting for permission
From a partner, boss, or God.

It's not in the job.
It's not in the pay.
It's not in applause
Or what people say.

It's in the moment you draw your line.
The second you say, "This choice is mine."
It's waking up and owning your day.
It's walking out and choosing not to stay.

It's saying no without guilt in your chest.
It's making decisions that feel like rest.
It's knowing you don't need to be understood
To still do what you know is good.

You won't always be clapped for.
You might stand alone.
But real freedom starts
When you build your own tone.

Independence isn't noise.
It's not about fame.
It's quiet conviction
That doesn't need a name.

So stop waiting for a crown or a script to frame it.
You don't get independence by asking for it. You have to claim it.

*Life is a trade fair. But unfortunately, the trade isn't fair.*

You give your all,
They give you half.
You show up with soul,
They respond with a laugh.

You play by the rules,
They skip the line.
You wait your turn,
They jump ahead just fine.

You love hard.
You care deep.
You stay loyal.
You lose sleep.

And still, it doesn't always
come back the same.
Effort doesn't guarantee you
will win the game.

You'll see the lazy get lucky,
The dishonest succeed,
The loud get heard,
While the kind still bleed.

But that's the truth they
don't always share.
Life rewards, yes, but not
always fair.

Some trades cost more than
they show.
Some rewards take longer to
grow.
Some people win by cutting
the line.
Some learn patience and
wait for their time.

You can't control who plays
what hand.
But you can choose where
you stand.

So trade your energy where
it's matched, not drained.
Trade your love where it's
seen, not strained.

Trade your worth like it's
gold, not spare.
Because life may be a trade
fair.
But unfortunately, the trade
isn't fair.

***People don't always change. Sometimes, you just start seeing them clearly.***

You thought they were kind.
You thought they were true.
You filled in the blanks
With the version you knew.

You explained the silence.
You softened the tone.
You carried the hope
That they'd eventually own.

But time has a way of pulling the thread,
And showing you truths you haven't yet read.

It's not that they flipped
Or turned overnight.
You just finally saw
What was always in sight.
That smile had cracks.
That praise felt thin.
That warmth was wrapped
In something dim.

Maybe you outgrew the lens you wore.
Maybe you couldn't unsee anymore.

It hurts when the curtain finally falls.
When you realize the echo wasn't your call.

But it's not betrayal to accept what's real.
It's not hate to say what you feel.

You're not bitter.
You're just no longer blind.
You finally see what was always aligned.

So don't chase who they were in your version dearly.
People don't always change.
Sometimes, you just start seeing them clearly.

***Some blessings come dressed as breakdowns.***

It fell apart
The plan. The pace.
The version of you
That fit that place.

You lost the role.
You lost the fight.
You sat alone
On sleepless nights.

And for a while, it felt like the end,
Like life had refused to bend.

You cursed the fall.
You questioned why.
You grieved the dream
That wouldn't fly.

But slowly, in that hollow space,
You found a deeper kind of grace.
A stillness you had never known.
A strength that grew when left alone.

You met yourself beyond the race,
Without the mask. Without the chase.
You built again, but not the same.
You played a freer, wilder game.

Turns out the fall was not a flaw.
It was a mirror, it broke the draw.

And what you had called a breakdown then,
Was the start of something that wouldn't have been.

So the next time it feels like life's gone wrong,
Wait. Breathe. You might be strong
Because not all gifts wear golden crowns.
Some blessings come dressed as breakdowns.

***You're not behind. You're just on a different clock.***

Some land their dream job at 25.
Some still don't know what they want at 35.
Some meet their person on a dating app.
Some meet them after a divorce and a nap.

Some go viral in a week.
Some build quietly, brick by brick.
Some hit milestones like a checklist.
Some take the scenic route and still feel rich.

And still, we scroll.
We compare.
We panic.
As if success is some mechanical magic.

But clocks don't tick the same for all.
And timelines are not gospel at all.

You're not late.
You're not lost.
You're not less.
You're just living a story that's still in progress.

Let them peak early.
Let them get loud.
You're growing roots that don't need a crowd.

So stop asking if you're on time or off track.
You were never behind. There's nothing to come back.

You're still becoming. You're still unlocking.
You're not behind. You're just on a different clock.

***What if everything is happening for you, but not in your language?***

You prayed for growth,
And got discomfort.
You wished for peace,
But life gave effort.

You asked for strength,
And met delay.
You wanted answers,
Life sent grey.
You begged for signs,
For skies that speak.
But all you heard
Was silence that creaked.

So you questioned the path.
You doubted the plan.
You thought, "If this is for me,
Why can't I understand?"

But what if blessings don't always arrive in words?
What if healing shows up through things that hurt?
What if the lesson came without the script?
What if the shift was in what you skipped?

You're waiting for clarity wrapped in gold.
But some truths are whispered, not boldly told.

You might be growing, just not out loud.
You might be rising, beneath the cloud.

So pause the panic.
Rethink the damage.
What if everything is happening for you,
But not in your language?

***Don't confuse silence with peace.***
***Sometimes, they're opposites.***

Silence can heal.
But silence can hide.
It can feel like calm,
While a storm brews inside.

You say nothing to avoid a fight.
You bottle it up to "keep things light."
You walk on eggshells,
Smile on cue,
Convincing the world
That you're okay too.

But there's a silence that soothes,
And one that suffocates.
There's a quiet by choice,
And a quiet that breaks.

Peace isn't just the lack of sound.
It's how it feels when no one's around.
It's not about stillness or shutting the door.
It's feeling safe,
Not needing to roar.

So ask yourself when your world feels tight:
Is this silence truth, or just a flight?

Because sometimes what looks like calm on the surface,
Is just suppressed hurt, doing its service.

You deserve more than a muted existence.
You deserve peace, not passive resistance.

So don't shrink your voice just to coexist.
Don't confuse silence with peace. Sometimes, they're opposites.

***Most people don't fear change. They fear not being in control of it.***

Change isn't the enemy.
It's the feeling of free fall.
It's not knowing when
Or where you'll land at all.

We say we fear change,
But that's not quite true.
We fear the shifts
That happen without our cue.

We're okay with growth
If we set the pace.
We're fine with risk
When we choose the race.

It's the sudden turn.
A plan gone rogue.
The chapter that starts
Before the last one's closed.

Control is comfort.
Control feels neat.
It tricks the mind
Into feeling complete.

But life has a way
Of moving the gate.
It doesn't wait
Till you feel great.

So maybe it's not change
That stirs the pit.
Most people don't fear change.
They fear not being in control of it.

***If you can't change the story, change your role in it.***

Not every script will bend your way.
Not every scene lets you have a say.
Some plots are fixed, no matter the fight.
Some endings just won't turn out right.

You can't always rewrite the past.
Can't force the pace, can't make it last.
But you don't have to keep playing the part
That keeps breaking your back and your heart.

Maybe you were the helper,
The glue, the guide.
But now it's time,
To step aside.

Maybe you were the one who stayed,
Who gave too much,
Who always paid.

So flip the role.
Change the gear.
Be the one who chooses clear.

Sometimes power,
Is not in the plot,
But in saying,
"This is not my spot."

You don't need the story to fully commit.
If you can't change the story, change your role in it.

***The biggest shift isn't in the situation. It's in your stance.***

Sometimes the problem doesn't go away.
The job is the same, the bills still stay.
The people don't change, the noise doesn't mute.
And yet something starts to feel less acute.

Because one day, you stop reacting the same.
You stop playing the blame game.
You stop waiting for them to come through,
And start asking what you're willing to do.

The shift isn't always loud or grand.
Sometimes it's just the way you stand.

It's going from "Why me?" to "Try me."
From "This is unfair" to "What can this teach me?"
It's walking into the fire with open eyes.
It's knowing you'll rise even if no one apologizes.

The world may not soften or suddenly dance.
The biggest shift isn't in the situation. It's in your stance.

***You don't need to escape the storm. You need to learn where to stand.***

When life gets loud and plans go wrong,
And every hour feels too long,
When people change and nothing's clear,
And even your own voice feels hard to hear,

You'll feel the urge to run away,
To pause it all, to skip the day,
To fix, to fight, to change the land,
But maybe, first, just try to stand.

Not all storms are meant to flee.
Some teach you who you're meant to be.
Some test your roots, some clear the air.
Some leave you stronger for standing there.

It's not about fixing all you see.
It's about finding calm in who you can be.

So the next time chaos takes command,
You don't need to escape the storm.
You need to learn where to stand.

***Reality isn't what happens. It's what you notice.***

The world isn't black or white.
It's not fixed. It's not fair.
It's painted by what
You choose to be aware.

The same moment can break
you,
Or build you instead.
It depends on the story
You tell in your head.

Is it failure? Or is it a start?
Is it rejection? Or redirection
from heart?
Is it silence that hurts?
Or peace you've not met?
Is it being stuck?
Or you're just not there yet?

Perspective is power,
And you hold the lens,
To label the loss,
To rewrite the ends.

Some see mess.
Others see meaning.
Some chase more.
Others find leaning.

So before you decide what
your life has become,
Ask if you've noticed the rise
or the run.
Because what you see shapes
how you feel,
And what you focus on
becomes what's real.

Not every truth will knock or
shout.
Some truths live in what you
tune out.

So look again.
Look with choice.
Reality isn't what happens.
It's to what you give voice.

# CHAPTER II

# THE INNER GAME

***You weren't overreacting. You were just reacting to everything at once.***

You got teary in a Zoom call.
Blanked out mid-pitch.
Snapped at a friend
Over one small glitch.

And then came the guilt,
"Why am I like this?"
But it wasn't just that moment.
It was the hundred you missed.

It was waking up tired,
And sleeping with stress.
The boss who expects,
And the inbox that's a mess.

It was skipping chai
To chase a deadline.
It was scrolling at night
To feel halfway fine.

It was too many tabs
Open in your head.
Too many dreams
That you quietly fed.

Like the crow and the pot,
But instead of more height,
Your pebbles just pushed,
The water out of sight.

You weren't dramatic.
You weren't weak.
You were just holding
What you couldn't speak.

So the next time you break
Without a cue or a front,
Remember:
You weren't overreacting.
You were just reacting to
everything at once.

***You know the answer in your gut. You always do.***

They'll tell you to wait.
To think it through.
To make a list, then make list two.

They'll ask for logic, charts, and signs.
They'll want your truth to fit their lines.

But clarity doesn't shout in your face.
It shows up softly, in a quiet space.
In the tightness you feel when you say "yes" but mean "no."
In the gut drop when it's time to let go.

It's there in the job that looks good but feels wrong.
In the friendship that's lasted a little too long.
In the smile you fake,
The sleep you lose,
The dream that keeps whispering, "You have to choose."

Still, you doubt. Still, you delay,
Hoping the noise will take it away.
But no one can see what you're here to become.
No one else hears the beat of your drum.

You think you need time.
You think you need signs.
But deep down, the truth's been crossing your mind.

You already know what you need to do.
You're just hoping the answer is something new.

But it's not.
It never is.

The hardest part is not "knowing."
It's "trusting" what you already know.

You know the answer in your gut.
You always do.

***You CAN tell your mind to STOP.***

It spins,
It loops,
It rewinds the pain,
Runs old stories through new frames again.

It asks:
What if you stayed?
What if you fought?
What if you said what you never thought?

Your mind builds tunnels with no end in sight.
It keeps you awake in the middle of the night.

A word someone said in a passing tone,
Becomes a mountain you climb alone.
A look. A pause. A text unread,
Becomes a storm inside your head.

But you are not your racing thoughts.
You are not the web your mind has caught.
You are the breath beneath the noise.
The stillness that always holds the choice.

You don't need to believe every voice you hear.
You don't need to drown in every fear.

You can pause.
You can breathe.
You can break the loop.
You can step outside the endless scoop.

Say it out loud.
Say it soft.

You don't run me.
You're just a thought.

And like a cloud that loses shape on top,
You can tell your mind to stop.

***Are you thinking over it or overthinking it?***

There's a fine line,
Between reflection and spiral,
Between looking for clarity,
And losing your arrival.

You tell yourself you're
processing,
Weighing every side.
But deep down you know
You're just trying to hide.

You've played out the scene
A hundred ways in your head:
What you could've said,
What they should've said
instead.

And now it's not the moment
That's hurting your chest.
It's the meaning you've
stitched,
And the loops that don't rest.
Sometimes the problem
Isn't what went wrong.
It's the replays you run
All night long.

You're not seeking answers.
You're stuck in the spin.
Not moving forward,
Not tuning in.

So pause the pattern.
Drop the script.
Not everything needs
To be so tightly gripped.

You don't need a solution
That's perfectly lit.
Ask yourself again:
Are you thinking over it or
overthinking it?

***Finding calm in the chaos is the only way to deal with it. And you can only find it within you.***

The traffic doesn't stop when you need a break.
The world doesn't pause for your heartache.
The group chat keeps pinging.
The bills pile too.
And your thoughts run faster than they used to do.

You wait for a gap, a moment to breathe,
For things to slow down, for life to ease.
But calm doesn't come from a quiet street.
It begins the moment you drop the heat.

You find it by stepping away for a while,
By breathing in deep without forcing a smile.
By facing the ache you pretend isn't there,
And letting your heart know you're still aware.

You find it in sips of water between two calls.
In saying no. In not taking it all.
In long walks. In deep sighs. In letting things slide.
In knowing not everything needs to collide.

It's not about silence or perfect flow.
It's choosing to center when you can't control the show.

The chaos may roar,
But you hold the clue:
The calm you seek is already in you.

***Sometimes we don't push a rock out of our way thinking it might not move. But if we don't push it, it will not move.***

You size it up before you try.
It looks too big, too fixed, too high.
You tell yourself, "What's the point?" and stay.
And that's how most dreams drift away.

You hesitate once, and then again.
You play out failure in your brain.
You wait for signs, for strength, for proof.
But the only way out is to test the truth.

Because what if it moves with a little shove?
What if it shifts when you rise above?

You won't know what's possible if you stand still.
Sometimes, what blocks you obeys your will.

The path won't clear just because you groove.
If you never push it, it will never move.

***Cribbing only increases your problems. If you've got a problem, either focus on solving it, or move on.***

You talk about it once.
Then twice. Then more.
Till the problem becomes
Louder than before.

You replay what happened.
You repeat every line.
But not once do you ask,
"How do I realign?"

You tell ten people.
You stay in the loop.
And the more you stew,
The deeper the soup.

Complaining feels good,
But it won't clear the mess.
It feeds the chaos
And doubles the stress.

So either pick up the tools
And fix what you can,
Or step away softly
And make a new plan.

Your peace is the thing
You must act upon.
Solve what you can,
Or move on.

***Have you ever made a decision, before you made the decision?***

You said you'd think about it,
Weigh the pros and cons,
Sleep on it for a week,
And talk to everyone.

But deep down,
You already knew.
You just didn't want
That knowing to be true.

So you waited. You stalled.
You made a list or two.
But your gut had whispered
What you needed to do.

Because sometimes the heart
Decides before the mind.
And clarity comes
Before permission to find.

The delay isn't doubt.
It's fear in disguise.
The moment you choose
Is when you stop telling lies.

So if the answer is loud,
But you're still in suspense,
Ask yourself:
Are you choosing,
Or just waiting for it to make more sense?

***You're always a newbie until you're not.***

You fumble at first.
You ask too much.
You Google things
That others do by touch.

You feel like a fraud.
You hope they don't see
That you're figuring it out
While pretending to be.

But everyone starts,
Right where you stand.
Uncertain. Awkward.
A little unplanned.

And then one day,
Without warning or sign,
You're the one others
Look to for the line.

You give advice.
You trust your gut.
You stop saying,
"Am I good enough?"

The shift is slow,
But always true.
What once felt big,
Now moves through you.

There's no grand moment.
No confetti shot.
You're just a newbie,
Until you're not.

***The loudest part of growth is usually silent.***

It's skipping the fight
That used to begin.
It's letting them win,
But feeling the win.

It's sitting alone
Without reaching out.
It's trusting your step
Without needing a shout.

It's saying no
Without guilt or pause.
It's choosing peace
Without needing applause.

Growth isn't loud.
It's calm. It's defiant.
The loudest part of growth
Is usually silent.

***Most self-doubt isn't yours. It's inherited.***

You were raised to be careful,
To color inside the line,
To pick the safer subject,
Not to fall out of line.

You were taught to choose stability
Over chasing what feels true.
Not because they didn't love you,
But because the world scared them too.

Their fears became your inner voice,
Telling you to pause, not play,
To second-guess the leap,
And take the longer way.

But what if that doubt
Was never yours to keep?
What if it's their voice
That lulls your dreams to sleep?

That hesitation in your chest
Isn't always intuition.
It might be protection
Wearing the mask of inhibition.

So trace the voice.
Ask who it sounds like.
And hand it back, gently,
The fear, the mic.

So the next time doubt tells you what not to do,
Ask:
Is this mine,
Or what they passed through?

***You don’t lack motivation.
You lack meaning.***

You've tried waking up at 5.
You've made the to-do lists.
You've read the books that talk of grind
And chasing life with fists.

But still you snooze the alarm.
Still you scroll and stall.
Not because you're lazy,
But because it doesn't call.

Motivation isn't magic.
It's not about hype.
It's the fire that burns,
When something feels right.

The problem isn't willpower.
Or hustle. Or drive.
It's doing things
That don't make you feel alive.

When you know your "why"
You won't need to fake it.
You'll move even when tired,
Because your soul wants to make it.

So don't chase goals
That mean nothing inside.
Chase what moves you.
That's where fuel hides.

You're not broken.
You're not leaning.
You don't lack motivation.
You lack meaning.

***Just because you're used to the weight doesn't mean it's not heavy.***

You've carried it for so long,
It almost feels like skin.
The expectations. The pressure.
The noise within.

You don't flinch anymore
When things pile high.
You just breathe, smile,
And say, "I'll try."

But endurance is not ease.
And silence is not peace.
You've just mastered the art
Of making the ache look the least.

Maybe it's the job
That drains your spark.
Or the role you play
That leaves a mark.

Maybe it's being the strong one
Every time things fall.
But even pillars crack
When they hold it all.

So don't confuse strength
With never feeling strain.
You're allowed to say:
"This is pain."

You don't have to break
To put it down gently.
Just because you're used to the weight
Doesn't mean it's not heavy.

***Self-worth isn't proven. It's remembered.***

You don't have to earn it
With late nights and yeses.
You don't need to bleed
To silence the guesses.

It's not in your title,
Not in your feed,
Not in the speed
At which you succeed.

You were enough
Before they asked for more.
Before the gold stars.
Before keeping score.

You're not a brand.
You're not a pitch.
You're not here
To scratch their itch.

You forgot your worth
Because they sold you doubt,
Taught you to dim
What wanted to shout.

But this isn't a test.
You've already passed.
You were born whole,
You just forgot that fast.

You came here full
Of fire and fight.
You don't need permission
To take up your light.

You're not here to beg to be
entered.
Self-worth isn't proven,
It's remembered.

***If you need to shrink to fit, it's not your space.***

If you're biting your tongue
More than you speak,
If you hide your strong
To come off as weak,

If you laugh a little softer
Just to blend in,
And wear a new mask
Each place you've been,

If you're walking on glass
Just to feel seen,
And dimming your truth
To keep things clean,

Then pause and ask:
Is this your race?
Or are you just running
To keep their pace?

You were not made
To be trimmed or erased.
Or molded to fit
Where you feel misplaced.

Real spaces won't flinch
When you stand tall.
They'll widen the room
Or break the wall.

So the next time you're shrinking
To feel embraced,
Remember this line:
It's not your space.

***If your boundaries upset them, that's the truth working.***

Not everyone likes the new
you,
The one who says no
Instead of nodding through.

The one who doesn't explain
Every need, every line,
Who doesn't trade peace
To keep things "fine."

You'll hear:
"You've changed."
"You're too much."
"You're distant."
"You've lost touch."

But what you've really done
Is stopped bending,
Stopped blending,
Stopped pretending.

You've drawn a line
And called it yours.
Closed old wounds
That stayed as doors.

And if that stings them
More than it should,
It's not you being cruel.
It's you being good.

Because truth is not always
Neat and smooth.
It shakes the ground
When it starts to move.

So let them flinch
And call it hurting.
If your boundaries upset them,
That's the truth working.

***Self-trust is built every time you choose your voice over their validation.***

You weren't born second-guessing.
That came later.
With every "Are you sure?"
And every "You should be greater."
You learned to check the mirror
Through someone else's eyes.
To seek approval
Before you tried.

You started asking others
What only you could know,
And got addicted to the nod
Before you let yourself grow.

But truth isn't voted on.
And courage isn't crowd-approved.
You build it in quiet moments
Where only you are moved.

Like when you speak,
Even if your voice shakes.
Or walk away,
Even if your heart breaks.

Like when you trust the pull,
Without asking why.
Or stop performing,
And choose to cry.

That's when the shift begins.
That's when you stop faking.
Self-trust is built
Every time you choose your voice over their validation.

***You don't need to explain your healing to those who benefit from your wounds.***

Some people liked you broken.
Not out of cruelty.
But because your cracks,
Made their flaws feel free.

You were easier to manage,
When you kept it in.
Easier to like
When you let them win.

So when you started to rise,
When you drew the line,
When you stopped saying sorry
For simply wanting time,
It made them uncomfortable.
Because healing shifts the
script.
And those who were handed
power,
Feel it has slowly slipped.

They'll call you selfish.
Say you've changed.
Say you've forgotten
The rules they arranged.

But here's the truth
That cuts through the noise.
You were never here
To play their decoy.

Your growth is yours,
Not theirs to assess.
Their comfort is not
Your progress test.

So stop explaining
To those who watched you
break.
You don't owe healing
To the ones who fed the ache.

***The breakthrough often comes right after you stop pretending you're fine.***

You keep it together in public,
Master of the nod and grin.
But behind that well-timed smile
Is a war you never let begin.

You've been busy being okay,
Fixing everyone else's storm.
Holding space for the world,
While your own pain took form.

But healing doesn't start
In silence or disguise.
It begins in the moment
You stop telling lies.

Lies like:
"I'm good."
"I've got this."
"It's no big deal."

When the truth is:
You're tired.
You're breaking.
You need time to feel.

Because cracks don't close
By acting like they're not there.
They open wider
When you fake that you don't care.

Strength isn't in pretending.
It's in saying, "I'm not fine."
That's when it shifts.
That's your sign.

The fall feels sharp,
But the climb is divine.
The breakthrough often comes
Right after you stop pretending you're fine.

***Sometimes growth is choosing not to react.***

You used to jump at every jab.
Fire back, prove a point,
Explain yourself
Until the air felt tight.

You'd match their heat
Word for word.
Try to be louder
Just to be heard.

But growth is not louder.
It's not sharp replies.
It's learning when
To let silence rise.

It's the moment you breathe
Instead of bite.
When you walk away,
Not to avoid, but to choose what's right.

It's knowing your peace
Isn't up for trade.
Not for power,
Not for shade.

It's seeing the bait
And letting it be.
Because not every battle
Deserves a "me."

So the next time drama
Knocks at your door,
Don't always answer
Like you did before.

Sometimes growth
Is choosing not to react.

***Peace doesn't come from winning. It comes from not needing to prove you can.***

You don't always need to argue your case.
You don't need to win just to save face.
You don't need to show them how strong you are
By entering every tug-of-war.

You've spent years trying to be understood,
To prove your worth,
To prove you're good,
To prove you're right,
To prove you belong.
But sometimes that need
Is what keeps you wrong.

Because peace doesn't come
From putting someone in their place.
It comes from choosing
Not to run that race.

It comes from knowing
That walking away
Isn't weakness.
It's wisdom at play.
That your energy
Deserves protection.
Not every battle
Needs correction.

Real strength is still
Not loud or grand.
Peace doesn't come from winning.
It comes from not needing to prove you can.

***Stop chasing consistency. Chase honesty.***

They told you to be one thing,
To stick to your lane,
To pick a version of yourself,
And never change.

But humans aren't headlines.
You're not a brand.
You're allowed to shift
Like footprints in sand.

Some days you're focused,
Some days you drift.
Some days you speak up,
Some days you sit.

You're not flaky
If you feel different today.
You're just honest enough
Not to fake your way.

Because what good is consistency
If it buries your truth?
What good is the mask
If it silences your roots?

Honesty isn't chaos.
It's clarity in disguise.
It's saying, "This is who I am,"
Beneath the compromise.

So stop editing yourself
For the sake of symmetry.
Stop chasing consistency.
Chase honesty.

***The work isn't to become your best self. It's to become your whole self.***

You've been told to aim
higher,
To improve, to refine,
To chase a version of you
That's perfect, that shines,
To fix the flaws,
To rise above,
To glow with grit,
And hustle with love.

But what if the goal
Isn't better, but real?
Not polishing the surface,
But learning to feel?

What if growth
Isn't always a climb?
But sitting with parts
You've silenced with time?

The fears. The mess.
The parts you've denied.
The stories you've buried.
The truths you hide.

Your wholeness isn't built
In just light or success.
It's in owning the shadows
You usually suppress.

It's not about perfection.
It's about depth.
It's meeting all versions
Of you that are left.

So don't chase the "best"
As if it's a shelf.

The work isn't to become your
best self.
It's to become your whole self.

# CHAPTER III

# WORK, WORTH & BURNOUT

***Burnout isn't about how much you're doing. It's about how little it means to you.***

You're checking the boxes,
Meeting the deadlines,
Showing up early,
Staying later than time.

From the outside,
You're doing great.
But inside?
You're running on an empty plate.

It's not the hours
That wear you thin.
It's pouring yourself
Into things you don't believe in.
Tasks that feel hollow.
Calls that drain.
Work that fills the calendar,
But starves the brain.

It's waking up tired
Before the day begins.
Because somewhere along the way,
You lost the "why" within.

Burnout doesn't ask,
"How much have you done?"
It whispers,
"When did this stop being fun?"

So look beyond your to-do list
And into your truth.
Does it light you up,
Or strip your youth?

Because burnout isn't about how much you're doing.
It's about how little it means to you.

***You're not tired of work. You're tired of being unseen.***

You show up.
You give more than asked.
You carry the load
Behind every task.
You stay back late,
Say yes on cue,
And somehow it still
Goes unnoticed too.

It's not the work
That's breaking you down.
It's doing it all
And still feeling drowned.
It's the smile no one sees,
The effort ignored,
The ideas dismissed,
The silence stored.

You're not asking for praise,
Or a standing ovation.
Just some honest
Recognition.

An "I see you,"
A "That mattered,"
Something to show
You weren't just scattered.

But the meetings move on,
The credits go wide,
And you're left questioning
Your own stride.

So the next time you say,
"I think I'm done,"
Ask yourself:
"Or am I just run
By a loop that says
I need to be seen
To feel like I matter
In this whole machine?"

You're not tired of work.
You're tired of being unseen.

***Creating starts with listening. If you don't understand the ones you're creating for, you can't add value. And you'll be irrelevant before you even start.***

You've got a voice.
A vision. A spark.
You want to make something
That leaves a mark.

A reel.
A product.
A post with punch.
But are you sure
You've heard their hunch?

Do you know what they need?
What they crave?
What keeps them stuck?
What helps them stay brave?

Because creating isn't shouting
Into a room.
It's sensing the silence
Before there's a boom.

It's tuning in
Before turning loud.
It's reading between the lines,
Not just pleasing the crowd.
The best creators
Don't just speak.
They listen.
They observe.
They tweak.

They know
Virality fades
But resonance stays.
And impact comes
From empathy-led ways.
So before you craft,
Record or write,
Ask who you're serving,
And if you got it right.

Because the goal isn't likes,
Or going viral overnight.
It's making something
That truly lands right.

Creating starts with listening.
That's how you earn your light.

*Letting someone do their job is a very tough job. Most leaders can't do it.*

You call it delegation,
But you can't let go.
You assign the task,
And still run the show.

You check every comma,
You hover and steer.
You say you trust them,
Then interfere.

But trust isn't built
Through constant correction.
It's built when you stop
Needing perfection.

Leadership isn't
Doing it all.
It's knowing when
To take the fall.

To back your team
When things go wrong.
To hold the silence
And still feel strong.

It's not about knowing
More than the rest.
It's about making space
So they can be their best.

If you can't let them own it,
You haven't led.
You've just managed
With your ego instead.

Because letting someone do
their job
Isn't easy.
It's brave.
And most leaders
Never learned how to behave.

***Don't feel guilty.***
***You're doing your best.***

You missed a call.
You snapped too fast.
You forgot to reply.
You didn't outlast.

Now you're replaying
Every move, every mess.
Dragging yourself
Through silent stress.

But pause.
Look closer.
There's no villain here.
Just someone tired,
Trying to steer.

You've been carrying more
Than most can see,
And still showing up
Quietly, steadily.

Some days are chaos,
Some days a blur,
And doing your best
Won't always look sure.

But guilt won't help.
It won't fix or bless.
It only adds weight
To an already-full chest.

So take a breath.
Forgive the rest.
Don't feel guilty.
You're doing your best.

***No job is ever big or small. Your vision is.***

You think some roles are beneath you,
Too routine, too slow.
You wait for that "big break,"
Before you really show.

But meaning isn't hiding
In a corner-office chair.
And impact isn't louder
Just because the title's rare.

Every job can build you
If you choose to be built.
Even the mundane
Can sharpen your skill.

Folding clothes.
Answering calls.
Running errands.
Painting walls.

It all adds up
If your eyes can see
That greatness begins
In doing it fully.

So don't judge the task.
Judge how you show up.
With half-hearted effort,
Or with a vision filled up.

Because the job doesn't shrink.
It's your lens that's small.

***Motivation looks good when life's just okay. But when life is in shambles, the first person you want to punch is the one trying to motivate you.***

When someone's world is falling apart,
Don't rush to hand them a quote.
Don't lace up your pep talk
And shove it down their throat.

Not every silence needs a speech.
Not every wound wants a cure.
Sometimes, they just need
To sit with what's unsure.

Because when someone can't breathe,
You don't offer them a race.
You sit beside them.
You slow the pace.

Motivation isn't a medicine
You throw at every bruise.
It's something they reach for,
Not something you choose.

Let them be angry.
Let them cry.
Let the walls fall.
Don't ask why.

If you really care,
Don't try to inspire.
Just stay close,
Until they're ready to rise higher.

Because when life's in shambles,
The kindest thing you can do
Is not push them to be strong,
But let them just be true.

***Don't try to solve everything in one day, but do (try to) solve it one day.***

Some days feel like a tangled thread,
Too many worries in your head.
Health, heartbreak, unpaid dues,
Promises broken, paths you didn't choose.

It piles up fast, the weight, the dread.
You want to fix it all instead.
But healing doesn't happen in a sprint.
It's slow, it's quiet, often without a glint.

One meal cooked.
One text sent.
One truth faced.
One hour well spent.

You don't climb out in a single leap.
You rise in inches, out of the deep.
One breath. One choice. One kind reply.
One soft "no." One honest "why."

You're not behind. You're not too late.
You don't need to carry the full world's weight.
You just need to start, in your own way.

Don't try to solve everything in one day.
But do try to solve it, one day.

***If you're doing something for someone, either do it properly or don't do it at all.***

Don't do it for credit.
Don't do it for show.
Don't do it to say,
"I told you so."

Don't help and then hover.
Don't give and then count.
Don't sugarcoat favors
And bill the amount.

If you care, then care.
If you commit, then stay.
If you're not all in,
Get out of the way.

Fake help drains more
Than no help ever could.
It's dressed-up control
Parading as good.

Don't act like a hero
When you're here to score.
Kindness that's loaded
Is kindness no more.

So keep your ego.
Keep your pity call.
Do it with intent
Or don't do it at all.

***Hustle becomes harmful when rest feels like guilt.***

You cancel breaks like they're bad behavior.
As if slowing down
Means you've lost your flavor.

You check your phone
While you eat your meal.
You scroll through tasks
Instead of how you feel.

You wear "busy" like a badge,
But deep down, you're spent.
You forget what's joy
Without deadlines met.

Rest isn't a reward.
It's fuel.
It's not a sign of slacking.
It's what keeps you whole.

But somewhere, you linked worth to output,
To burning out,
Without calling it burnout.
To grinding, climbing, proving, hiding.
To doing everything
Except unwinding.

So here's your truth:
You don't owe exhaustion to your ambition.
You don't need to bleed to earn permission.

If sitting still makes you feel unfit,
That's not drive.
That's damage. Admit it.

Because hustle becomes harmful
When rest feels like guilt.

***Recognition isn't motivation. It's medicine.***

People aren't asking for the
moon.
They're asking to be seen.
To not be invisible
In the machine.

You think they'll stay
motivated
Because of paychecks and
deadlines.
But humans don't run
On silence and guidelines.

That intern who stayed late?
That manager who took the
fall?
That teammate who always
shows up?
They're not robots.
They feel it all.

You say, "It's their job."
Sure, it is.
But so is yours
To notice.
To thank.
To uplift.

Recognition isn't a bonus.
It's as basic as hygiene.
It's what keeps people
From falling between the
unseen.

Say "I saw what you did."
Say "That mattered."
Say "You make a difference."
And mean it.

Because without it,
Good people quit.
Not always on paper,
But quietly, bit by bit.

So if you lead,
Then lead like you mean it.
Make people feel
Like they aren't just a cog,
But a part of the dream in it.

Recognition isn't motivation.
It's medicine.
And sometimes, you're the one
Holding the prescription.

***Doing more is not the same as doing what matters.***

You crossed off ten tasks,
But did you move the needle?
You stayed busy all day,
But did it mean anything real?

You replied to emails.
Sat in calls.
Switched tabs.
Juggled walls.

But if you're honest,
Did anything shift?
Or did you just run
To avoid the drift?

Busyness looks productive,
But it often masks fear
Of choosing what matters,
Of getting clear.

Because doing what matters
Isn't always fast.
It requires focus
And letting go of the past.

You'll need to say no
To the noise that flatters,
And get uncomfortable
With what actually matters.

So check your list.
Then check your gut.
Did today bring you closer,
Or just keep your hands shut?

Because doing more
Is not the same
As doing what matters.

***Every yes at work is a no somewhere else.***
***Choose wisely.***

You said yes to the extra call,
Yes to the weekend grind,
Yes to staying back
Even when your body
declined.

Not because you loved the
chaos,
But because you thought you
should.
Because that's what the hungry
did:
They worked harder than they
could.

But every yes has a price.
Every stretch has a cost.
And sometimes what you gain
in output,
You lose in what you've lost.

Like dinner with family,
Sleep that heals,
Walks that ground,
Joy that feels.

Work isn't the villain,
But it should never be
The place where your worth
Goes to earn its fee.

Say yes when it fuels you.
Say yes when you grow.
Say yes when it aligns
With the life you want to
know.

But when it's hollow,
When it steals your peace,
It's okay to pause,
It's okay to release.

Because every yes at work
Is a no somewhere else.
So choose wisely,
And don't lose yourself.

***You can love your work and still want a break from it.***

Loving what you do
Doesn't make you a machine.
It means your heart is in it,
But your body still needs a routine.

You can wake up excited
And still feel drained by noon.
You can give your best
And still crave a slower tune.

To feel tired is human.
Even joy takes a toll.
And giving your all
Still needs a whole.

There's a difference between being done
And just needing a pause.
Even passion needs breathing room.
Even purpose finds clarity in a pause.

You're not betraying your dreams
By putting your feet up.
You're not less ambitious
For pouring a softer cup.

Rest doesn't mean you're over it.
It means you care enough to stay.
And the only way to last in love
Is to step back some days.

You can love your work
And still want a break from it.
That's not weakness.
That's wisdom. Admit it.

***Climbing the ladder doesn't always mean you're headed somewhere better.***

You kept your head down.
Played the game.
Chased the next title.
Built the name.

You said yes to more,
You stretched, you stayed,
Until success
Became a masquerade.

But higher isn't always happier.
Faster isn't always free.
And sometimes the view at the top
Isn't what you thought it would be.

Because not every ladder,
Leads to light.
Some just take you
Out of sight
From your values.
From your truth.
From the fire
You had in your youth.

So before the next rung
Feels like the prize,
Ask if it's worth
What your peace denies.

Progress isn't just
About the climb.
It's about asking
If it's still worth your time.

Climbing the ladder
Doesn't always mean
You're headed somewhere better.

***Respect doesn't come from titles. It comes from how you treat people with none.***

It’s easy to hold the door
For someone in a suit,
To nod at the one
Who wears power like a badge.

But the real test?
How you treat the ones
Without a tag.

The receptionist.
The cleaner.
The intern.
The help.

The ones who do the work
That often gets shelved.

Respect isn’t top-down.
It’s inside-out.
And it shows the most
When no one’s keeping count.

You may earn authority
From the seat you own.
But you earn respect
From the seeds you’ve sown.

So don’t measure your worth
By how high you’ve gone.
Measure it by how many
You lifted along.

Because respect doesn’t come from titles.
It comes from how you treat people with none.

*If your job drains you more than it grows you, it's too expensive.*

Not every cost shows up on a pay-slip.
Some show up in skipped meals
And sleepless nights,
In quiet tears during lunch breaks,
And fights that don't feel right.

You stay because it pays.
Because it looks good.
Because walking away
Feels worse than staying should.

But ask yourself:
What's it costing to stay?
Your health? Your time?
Your light each day?

You were meant to thrive,
Not just survive.
To grow where you work,
Not slowly come undone inside.

If it empties you more than it fills,
If it takes more than it returns,
Then no salary can justify
The version of you it burns.

You don't owe your life
To a job that steals your spark.
You owe it to yourself
To step out of the dark.

If your job drains you more than it grows you,
It's too expensive.
No title is worth that offensive.

***Leaders aren't the loudest ones in the room. They're the safest.***

You don't remember the boss
Who spoke the most.
You remember the one
Who made you feel seen,
Who noticed your silence,
Not just your screen.

A true leader doesn't need
To raise their voice to be
heard.
Their presence says more
Than any rehearsed word.

They don't lead with fear.
They lead with space.
With the kind of calm
That steadies the place.

They ask. They listen.
They wait their turn.
They don't set fires
Just to watch others burn.

You grow around them,
Not because you have to,
But because you want to.
You stay late,
Not from pressure,
But purpose.

It's not charisma
That makes them great.
It's that you breathe easier
In their weight.

Because leaders aren't
The loudest ones in the room.
They're the safest.
They're the bloom.

***Culture isn't what you write on the wall. It is what people whisper at lunch.***

The best ones don't walk in
To impress.
They walk in
To protect.
They don't just lead the room.
They hold it
With patience,
With steadiness,
With eyes that notice
What others overlook.

You feel safer when they're
around,
Not because they fix
everything,
But because you know
They won't let you drown.
They don't hover.
They have your back.
You take the leap
Because you trust they'll catch
the slack.

They don't shout directions.
They build trust in silence.
You make fewer mistakes,
Not from fear,
But from alignment.

You grow under them
Because they give you room.
You speak up
Because you know
They won't leave you in the
gloom.

It's not about charisma.
It's about care.
You move with more courage
Because you know they're
there.

Leaders aren't the loudest ones
in the room.
They're the safest.
The ones who make you feel
Like you're never alone in the
hardest.

***Getting paid well doesn't mean you're treated well.***

You can earn a fat check
And still feel small.
You can sit at the table
And still feel like the wall.

You can have perks and praise
But still walk on eggshells.
Because money buys silence,
Not respect as well.

They'll say you're lucky,
That others would kill for your spot.
But deep down, you know
This isn't the life you thought you'd got.

A good salary doesn't cover
The cost of dread,
Of being unheard,
Of bending your head.

Work isn't just about what you're paid.
It's about how you're made to feel each day.

So don't confuse being well compensated
With being well valued.
The two aren't the same.
And you know it
Because it weighs just like pain.

Getting paid well doesn't mean you're treated well.
It just means they can afford your hell.

***Your worth isn't in your output. It's in your insight.***

The world moves fast,
But wisdom takes time.
And the most valuable minds
Aren't just doing.
They're observing,
Learning,
Refining their climb.

You grow not just by shipping more,
But by seeing more,
By asking better questions,
By connecting dots others ignore.

It's not about how many things you finish,
But how deeply you understand.
Because insight builds the foundation
That speed alone can't withstand.

Great thinkers aren't born,
They're built,
Through moments of silence,
Through failures rebuilt,
Through listening closely
Before rushing to act.

Every experience,
Every pause,
Every setback,
Adds a layer to your impact.

So trust the slowness that teaches.
The stillness that sharpens your sight.
Because in a world obsessed with output,
Your true worth is your insight.

# CHAPTER IV

# PEOPLE YOU LOVE, PEOPLE WHO HURT

***Sometimes the best way to let them know you existed all this while, is to walk away.***

You spoke,
They heard noise.
You stayed,
They called it choice.

You showed up full,
They saw you small.
You gave your all,
They saw none at all.

But silence hits harder
When it walks out the door.
And absence, sometimes,
Says even more.

Not every exit
Is a sign you broke.
Some goodbyes
Are a power stroke.

You don't need noise
To make them see.
You just need
To set yourself free.

You're not leaving weak.
You're rising strong.
You were just in a room
Where you didn't belong.

So walk away,
Not to disappear,
But to remind them:
You were always here.

*When you're the one who always gives people strength, they forget that sometimes, you need it too.*

You're the rock.
The calm.
The call at 2 a.m.
The silent hand
That steadies them.

But when you bend
And break in two,
They blink like
They never knew.

Strong is a title
They give you fast.
So they forget
That it doesn't always last.

You're the lifeboat
In every storm.
But even anchors
Need to feel warm.

You hide the cracks.
You show the light.
But strength, too,
Should have the right
To say:
Not today,
I'm tired, I'm low.
I need someone
To help me grow.

You're not weak
For needing space.
Even heroes
Need a landing place.

So the next time
They forget your hue,
Remind them:
Strength needs strength, too.

*Be good. Create beautiful moments. For you really don't know which one could be the last. With them.*

Say the thing.
Take the call.
Hug them tighter.
Drop the wall.

Laugh too loud.
Stay up late.
Choose the joy
Before the fate.

We chase tomorrows.
Delay the now.
But life can switch
Without a vow.

That last goodbye
Won't come signed.
It'll show up quiet
And unlined.

So be the warmth,
The calm, the spark.
Be the light
Before it's dark.

Be good. Create beautiful moments.
For you really don't know which one could be the last. With them.

***Why does it affect you when people are winning the game you're not even playing?***

They'll play the game,
The tricks, the spin.
They'll gossip loud
And call it a win.

They'll count your steps,
Mock your grace,
Try to drag you
Into their race.

But you're not bait.
You're not their chess.
You don't need noise
To feel success.

Let them hustle
For the crown.
You're too busy
Holding it down.

Your peace
Is not their pawn.
And your focus?
Already moved on.

So the next time they plot
Or throw your name,
Ask yourself this
To exit the frame:

Why does it affect you
When people are winning
The game you're not even playing?

***When you try too hard to protect it, you end up destroying it.***

You hold it close.
Too close.
Like cupping water in your hands.
Shaking, tense.
Afraid to spill.
Afraid to lose.
You overthink.
You micromanage.
You wrap it in fear
And call it love.
You set rules
Where there should've been rhythm.
You build walls
To keep it safe,
But end up locking out the air.
You check the temperature
Before every word.
You dim yourself
Just so it won't burn.
But in trying to hold it all together,
You stop letting it breathe.

The truth?
Not everything needs guarding.
Some things grow
Only when left open.
Some bonds deepen
When you loosen the grip.
It's not neglect
To let it flow.
It's wisdom
To let it go.

Because sometimes,
The thing you're trying to save
Is suffocating
From how much you're trying.
When you try too hard to protect it,
You end up destroying it.

***Love at first sight, or love at "first vibe"?***

It's not the face.
It's not the fit.
It's how they make
Your soul commit.

It's not the height,
Or shoe-size talk.
It's how your mind
Goes off its clock.

It's not the hair,
Or jawline clean.
It's how you feel
Just in between.

When conversation flows
Without a plan,
And silence doesn't
Feel like a ban.

It's laughs that hit
All the spots.
It's "Tell me more"
Instead of "What?"

We've met the pretty,
And the smooth,
But vibe is something
You don't prove.

It's weirdly calm.
It's oddly light.
It feels like home.
It feels just right.

So save the looks.
Forget the hype.
We fall for people
With the right type…of vibe.

Love at first sight,
Or love at first vibe?
You already know
Which one's your tribe.

***Life is small. And holding on to grudges makes it smaller. Forgive. Forget. Move on.***

Life's already short.
No rewind, no redo.
So why waste time
Stuck on who hurt you?

You carry the weight,
But they walk free.
You replay the scene,
They lost the key.

Grudges don't fix.
They don't heal pain.
They just pour salt
Again and again.

You think holding on
Gives you control,
But it only shrinks
Your peace, your soul.

Forgiveness isn't weak.
It's setting fire
To the story
That made you tired.

Not for them,
But just for you.
So you can grow
Past what you knew.

Don't let anger
Be your view.
Don't let pain
Define what's true.

Let it go.
Let it slide.
You've got more love
On the other side.

Life is small.
Holding on to grudges makes it smaller.
Forgive. Forget. Move on.

***You always know it's a sign while you're ignoring it. Always.***

It starts as a nudge.
A feeling offbeat,
A whisper inside
You try to defeat.

You laugh it off.
Call it a phase.
But deep down you know
You're stuck in a haze.

The gut says go.
The heart says wait.
You stall your truth
And call it fate.

Red flags wave,
But you paint them white.
You stay in the dark
And call it light.

You scroll past signs.
You mute the sound,
Pretending peace
Can still be found.

But silence screams
When it's time to choose.
And what you ignore
Is what you lose.

Because deep in your bones,
Beneath the noise,
You always knew
You had the choice.

You always know it's a sign
While you're ignoring it.
Always.

***Some people have only one thing to offer: stress.***

They walk in loud,
But bring no peace.
Their chaos talks.
And joy? On lease.

Every text feels
Like a little fight.
Every meet
Drains your light.

It's always drama,
Never calm.
They show up
Like a ticking bomb.

You give them space,
They take your air.
You show them love,
They leave you bare.

It's not bad luck.
It's not a test.
Some people
Just bring stress.

No support.
No steady ground.
Just guilt and games
All year round.

You try to help.
You try to stay.
But peace should never
Feel this way.

So protect your vibe.
Protect your mind.
Not every bond
Is worth the grind.

***Is it really effort, if it ends?***

You said you tried.
You gave your all.
But the effort that quits
Isn't effort at all.

You called it love.
You called it fight.
But the real ones don't
Just lose the light.

If it mattered,
You'd still be there.
You'd break the wall.
You'd climb the stair.

You don't drop dreams
That were truly yours.
You knock again
On shut-down doors.

It's not called effort
When it times out fast.
It's not real fire
If it doesn't last.

Wanting is easy.
Trying is loud.
But staying when it's hard,
That's what makes you proud.

So no,
It's not effort
If you let it bend.
Because real effort
Doesn't end.

***It isn't easy to find what you love, but it is to find what you don't. That's where you start.***

Everyone's asking:
What's your thing?
Your dream?
Your spark?
Your inner zing?

But the truth is,
Most of us don't know.
And no one claps
When you're moving slow.

We talk of passion
Like it shows up loud.
A lightning flash
Above the crowd.

But love?
It sneaks.
It builds in layers.
Not just big wins
And viral prayers.

So if you don't know
What feels just right,
Start by cutting
What dims your light.

The jobs you dread.
The things you fake.
The tasks that suck
More than they make.

Each "no" you feel
Clears space for a "yes."
Each door you close
Removes the mess.

You don't find your love
By sitting still.
You find it by failing
With your will.

So stop chasing
Some grand chart.
It isn't easy to find what you
love,
But it is to find what you don't.
That's where you start.

***Some people love you, but only in ways that break you.***

They say the words.
They hold you tight.
But somehow,
Nothing feels quite right.

They show they care,
But not in peace.
Their kind of love
Comes with a lease.

It lifts you up,
Then cuts you down.
Gives you hope,
But lets you drown.

They love in ways
That wear you thin,
Where you always lose
And they always win.

It's love that stings,
But you stay still.
Because hurt that's known
Can feel like will.

You make excuses.
You play it cool.
But deep inside,
You feel the rule:

Love should never
Steal your voice.
It should never
Rob your choice.

So don't confuse
The words they say,
With how they make
Your soul decay.
Because yes,
Some people do love you.
But only
In ways
That break you.

***Sometimes, the person who saved you back then is the one holding you back now.***

They caught you once
When you were low.
They stayed when others
Let you go.

They gave you light
When days were dark,
And left a "forever"
On your heart.

You owe them much,
Or so it feels.
Their care back then
Still softly heals.

But time moves on,
And people change.
What once felt close
Can turn strange.

Their voice, once calm,
Now makes you shrink.
Their help feels heavy,
Makes you sink.

You keep them near
Out of old debt.
But every step
Feels like regret.

The truth is hard,
But here's the key:
Not all who helped
Are meant to be.

Some chapters end,
And that's okay.
You can love the past
And still walk away.

***Closure is a self-made thing. Stop waiting for their version.***

You wait for words
That may never come.
A sorry, a why,
A reason, some.

You hold the door
Just slightly wide,
Hoping they'll step in
And justify the tide.

You replay scenes.
You rewrite the end.
You think if they speak,
Your heart might mend.

But closure?
It's not their line to say.
It's not in the text
They forgot to send today.

It's you,
Deciding you've felt enough.
It's choosing peace
When things stay rough.

It's walking out
Without the bow.
It's letting go
Without the how.

Because waiting for them
Is staying stuck.
And you deserve
Much more than luck.

Their version
May never come through.
But you don't need theirs
To make it true.

***You didn't change. You just stopped apologizing for who you are.***

They say you've changed,
You're not the same.
But all you did
Was leave their game.

You spoke up loud.
Stood tall, stood clear.
Now suddenly,
You're "tough" and "weird."

But the truth is,
You've always been this way.
You just shrank yourself
To make them stay.

You laughed less loud.
You dimmed your spark.
You played it safe
To match their mark.

But masks get heavy,
And filters crack.
One day you snap
And don't look back.

Now they call it ego,
Call it pride.
But it's just that you
No longer hide.

You didn't switch.
You didn't stray.
You just stopped
Saying sorry everyday.

***Stop waiting for them to understand. Start choosing who does.***

You explain.
You break it down.
You shrink your truth
To fit their frown.

You replay words.
You soften tone.
You carry weight
That's not your own.

But not everyone
Will see your side.
Some just don't care.
Some won't even try.

You wait for them
To meet you there,
While losing sleep
In thin, cold air.

But understanding
Isn't begged.
It's found
In spaces safe,
On solid ground.

So stop twisting
To make them see.
You're not a puzzle.
You're just . . . free.

Don't chase the crowd
That mocks your core.
Choose the ones
Who ask for more.

***You don't have to hate them to walk away.***

Not every ending
Needs a fight.
Not every silence
Proves you're right.

Sometimes the love
Was real and true,
But just not meant
To carry through.

You shared the laughs.
You shared the pain.
But holding on
Won't bring more gain.

No shattered glass.
No final scream.
Just growing out
Of a shared dream.

You don't need anger
To let it go.
You don't need closure
Wrapped in a bow.

You can wish them well
And still move on.
You can care
And still be gone.

Because peace
Doesn't always stay.
And you don't have to hate them
To walk away.

***The ones who hurt you the most are usually the ones you gave the most access.***

It wasn't a stranger.
Not some face in the crowd.
It was someone you let in.
Someone you spoke of out loud.

You handed them the keys
To the parts you hide.
Told them the stories
You keep inside.

They knew the cracks,
The softest part.
They held the map
To your beating heart.

And that's why it cut,
Not just deep,
But clean.
Because they struck
Where you'd never seen.

You gave them access,
Not just space.
You let them close.
You moved at their pace.

But access isn't
Always earned.
And love, when mishandled,
Will always burn.

So no,
It wasn't weakness.
It was trust misplaced,
And a lesson in knowing
Who deserves what space.

***Emotional manipulation looks like concern on the surface.***

It starts with "I care."
A soft tone.
A warm stare.
But slowly,
You lose your air.

They question your moves.
They frame it as love.
But it feels more like
Being shoved.

You shrink.
They shine.
You fall in line.

That's not care.
That's control in disguise.

How to know?
When you feel small
For being whole.
When "support"
Starts taking a toll.

How to stop it?
Call it out.
Set the line.
Choose your truth
Over their design.

You don't need proof.
You need peace.

Emotional manipulation
Looks like concern on the surface.
But real love
Never makes you feel less on purpose.

***Sometimes, walking away is the kindest thing you can do, for both of you.***

You've talked it through.
You've bent. You've stayed.
You've watered roots
That never swayed.

You held on tight
Through every phase,
But love can't live
In an endless maze.

Some bonds don't break.
They slowly fade.
And staying just
Delays the blade.

It's not cold.
It's not cruel.
It's choosing truth
Over the rule.

Because forcing "forever"
When it's no longer true,
Only breaks
What once grew.

So take the step.
Let silence speak.
Sometimes the strongest
Look the least weak.

***The right people feel lighter, even on heavy days.***

Not every smile
Can lift your load.
Not every voice
Can clear the road.

But some just show up,
No big display.
And suddenly,
It's a softer day.

They don't fix it all,
Or say the right line.
But just being near
Feels like a sign.

You can cry.
You can pause.
You can say "I'm not okay."
And they stay,
Not out of duty,
But because they may.

No walking on eggshells.
No hiding the mess.
Just breathing easy,
In shared stress.

You don't feel judged.
You don't feel less.
They bring you calm,
Not second guess.

Because the right people
Don't just stay.
They feel lighter,
Even on heavy days.

***Some apologies won't come. Make peace anyway.***

Not every story
Gets a clean close.
Not every chapter
Ties up in prose.

Some leave mid-sentence.
Some drift away.
Some never look back,
Though you wish they'd stay.

But here's the magic:
You don't need their word.
You don't need closure
To feel unblurred.

You make peace
By choosing light.
By sleeping soft
On a solo night.

You stop the scroll.
You mute the pain.
You dance again
In your own lane.

You let it out,
Then let it go.
You stop rehearsing
What they'll never know.

You laugh without
Their name inside it.
You build a joy.
They can't divide it.

You heal by living,
By being okay,
Without the "sorry"
They'll never say.

***What you tolerate teaches them how to treat you.***

They cross the line,
You let it slide.
They shift the blame,
You run and hide.

You laugh it off.
You keep the peace.
But every time
You sign the lease.

Because silence says:
"This isn't wrong."
And staying quiet
Makes them strong.

You teach them rules
Without a word.
What you allow
Becomes the heard.

They learn from what
You let slip by,
From every look
You don't deny.

But here's the truth:
Respect's not asked.
It's shaped by what
You let pass.

So draw the line.
Say it plain.
You don't exist
To carry their pain.

You get what you stand for,
Or what you allow.
It starts with one "no."
It starts now.

What you tolerate
Teaches them how to treat
you.
So teach wisely.

***Boundaries are a love language too.***

It’s not a wall.
It’s not a fight.
It’s saying “This matters,”
And that feels right.

It’s not shutting out.
It’s letting in,
With clear lines drawn
On where you’ve been.

It’s “I need space,”
Not “I don’t care.”
It’s loving loud
By being fair.

It’s knowing when
To pause, to rest,
So what you give
Can be your best.

It’s not just hugs
Or words you say.
It’s how you hold
The noise at bay.

Because love isn’t
Just staying near.
It’s making someone
Feel safe and clear.

So don’t feel guilt
For what you do.
Boundaries are
A love language too.

***You can mourn someone who's still alive.***

They're breathing.
They laugh.
They post.
They glow.
But the bond you shared
Stopped long ago.

They didn't leave
In the usual way.
No final words.
No reason to stay.

Just distance,
Wearing a friendly face.
Just silence,
Filling up the space.

You see them move on,
Like you were a phase,
And grieve in moments,
You can't quite place.

You scroll past smiles
That don't include you.
You carry stories
They've outgrown too.

It's not always death
That makes us cry.
You can mourn someone
Who's still alive.

And that pain?
It's real.
It counts.
It stays.
But you'll heal too
In softer ways.

# CHAPTER V

# THE CHAOS OF CLARITY

*Sometimes the answer isn't complicated.*
*It's just uncomfortable.*

You ask again.
You spin the thread.
You look for signs
Inside your head.

You check with friends.
You overthink.
You write it down
In pen and ink.

But deep inside,
You always knew.
You just hoped
It wasn't true.

It's not some maze.
It's not some test.
It's just a truth
You liked less.

They don't care,
Or you outgrew.
Or maybe the love
Was never true.

But answers don't
Always wear disguise.
Some just hurt,
But they aren't lies.

You don't need
A hundred clues.
Just courage
To face what you'll lose.

Sometimes the answer
Isn't complicated.
It's just uncomfortable,
And that's what makes it hard.

***Sometimes clarity doesn't need more thinking. It just needs more honesty.***

You've turned it over
A thousand ways.
You've stayed up late
For countless days.

You've made pros and cons.
You've asked your crew.
You've looked for signs
You always knew.

But deep down,
You're not confused.
You're just afraid
Of what you'll lose.

It's not the mind
That's feeling stuck.
It's the truth you've hidden
To test your luck.

You know the vibe.
You've felt the shift.
But saying it out loud
Would cause a rift.

So you overthink
And call it wise.
But sometimes thought
Is just a disguise.

Because what you need
Isn't more debate.
It's the guts to say
What won't feel great.

Sometimes clarity
Doesn't need more thinking.
It just needs more honesty,
And the courage to follow it.

***The definition of a tough day changes with every tough day.***

Once it was traffic.
A missed call.
A plan that got cancelled.
A drop, not a fall.

A sharp word from someone.
A task gone astray.
That's all it took to ruin your day.

But then came the calls that made you sit down.
News that flipped your world upside down.
Days when the smile was just something you wore.
Nights when you cried, then showed up for more.

You didn't ask for it.
You didn't plan it.
But you bore it.
And bit by bit, you began to understand it.

Strength doesn't come from what you lift.
It comes from what you carry through every shift.

You're not the same as you were back then.
And that's why the scale keeps changing again.

What once broke you now just bends.
What once felt final now just ends.

So if today feels like too much to bear,
Know it's shaping the you who'll meet the next tear.

And one day you'll look back and say,
That wasn't the end.
That was just another tough day.

***You're allowed to outgrow your own beliefs.***

Once, you were sure.
So sure.
This is right.
This is wrong.
This is how it's done.
This is where I belong.

You held those thoughts
Like sacred ground.
You built your world
To match their sound.

But then came questions
That didn't sit still.
And truths that clashed
With your iron will.

You tried to ignore.
You tried to defend.
But deep down,
You felt the bend.

The path you praised
Started to shift.
The rules you swore by
Began to drift.

And you wondered,
Is this betrayal?
Is this weak?
Or just the soul
Trying to speak?

You feared letting go
Meant losing your name.
But growth never leaves you
Quite the same.
Because you're not here
To stay who you were.
You're here to evolve,
To blur, to stir.

The you of yesterday
Was not a mistake.
It brought you here.
But it doesn't have to stay
awake.

You can let go
Of thoughts that once fit.
You can release
What no longer sits.

You can believe new things.
Start again.
Because truth isn't final,
It's grown from within.

You're allowed to outgrow
your own beliefs.
That's not weakness.
That's becoming.

***If you stop explaining "why not" and start figuring "how", life will change.***

You say you're too old,
Or too new.
You don't have the time,
Don't have the crew.

You say the market's bad.
The timing's wrong.
You're not ready yet,
You don't feel strong.

So you explain.
And explain.
And explain again.
Until the dream gets buried beneath the "if" and "when."

But the truth is:
You're not stuck because you're lacking a way.
You're stuck because you keep finding reasons to stay.

Growth doesn't wait for a perfect plan.
It begins when you decide you can.
When the energy shifts from doubt to try.
From "What if I fail?" to "What if I fly?"

Ask different questions.
Better ones. Real ones.
"What's the first small step I can feel?"
"How can I move without knowing it all?"
"What if I rise every time I fall?"

Because action isn't loud.
It starts with a spark.
A shift in the story you tell in the dark.

So stop rehearsing every reason to bow,
And start figuring out your version of how.

***You're born to live, but you live to die.***

You're born with nothing
But breath in your lungs
And wonder in your eyes.
No shame.
No fear.
No need to apologize.

But slowly,
You start to shrink.
Not your body.
Your being.

You fear failing,
So you don't try.
You fear heartbreak,
So you don't fly.

You fear what they'll say,
So you mute your truth.
You fear being late,
So you rush your youth.

You fear not having enough,
Then fear losing what you do.
You fear being alone,
And still hide the real you.

And one day,
You wake up
And realize you've been alive
All this time,
But haven't really lived.
Because fear makes you
careful.
But too much
Makes you forget
What you came here for.
You weren't born
To be safe,
To be liked,
To play it light.

You were born
To crack open,
To dance with doubt,
To cry hard,
Laugh louder,
And figure it out.

And yes,
You live to die.
That's true.
But that's not the tragedy.
The tragedy
Is dying inside
While still making it through.

You're born to live,
But you live to die.
Don't let fear
Be the reason you never tried.

***There's always an ending and always a beginning. And it repeats. That's the only truth in life. Rest are all stories.***

Things end.
Things begin.
That's the rhythm.
That's the spin.

A job.
A phase.
A person.
A name.
You think it stays,
But nothing's the same.

You hold on tight
Until it slips.
You grieve, you grow.
The cycle flips.

You start again.
You learn the beat.
You fall.
You rise.
You rinse.
Repeat.
You tell yourself,
"This one will stay."
But even forever
Fades away.

The only truth
That time won't bend:
Every beginning
Meets its end.

And that's okay.
That's how we move.
That's how life
Finds its groove.

There's always an ending
And always a beginning.
And it repeats.
That's the only truth.
The rest
Are just stories.

***Every problem has a solution…unless it is your own.***

They call you
When things fall apart,
When they're lost,
Broken,
Or can't find their heart.

You listen.
You guide.
You give them light.
You make the mess
Look almost right.

You're the calm
In their confusion.
The logic
In their illusion.

And it's not fake.
You mean it all.
You hold their weight
So they don't fall.

But when it's you?
When you break down?
You go quiet.
You just drown.

The words disappear.
The clarity fades.
The fixer
Can't fix their own cascade.

You stare at the same patterns
You once untied.
But for yourself
You're blind inside.

Why?
Because when you help them,
You're not in it.
You see the edges.
You spot what's hidden.

But when it's yours,
It lives too close.
Your fears are louder
Than your inner force.

So here's the truth:
You're not broken.
You just need
What you've always spoken.

Someone who listens,
Who doesn't try to solve,
Who holds you,
While you evolve.

Maybe the answer
Isn't to solve alone.
Maybe even the healer
Needs a home.

Because yes,
You've solved every problem,
Except your own.
But maybe the answer
Is letting yourself be shown.

***Beauty lies in the eyes of the beholder, yes.***
***But also in the need.***

They say beauty
Lies in the eyes of the
beholder.
Yes.
But sometimes,
It lies in the need
Of the one looking.

Some don't see brilliance,
They see benefit.
They don't see talent,
They see a ticket.

Their compliments
Aren't observations.
They're strategies,
Calculated adorations.

They admire your charm,
But chase your clout.
They praise your work
When they need a way out.
To them, flattery
Is a handshake in disguise,
A soft whisper
To stay in your eyes.

They call it loyalty,
But it bends with gain.
They call you genius
Till the next can stake their
claim.

This isn't admiration.
It's positioning.
And if you don't see it,
It feels like winning.

But don't confuse
Echoes for truth,
Or loud praise
For actual proof.

***If you're happy and you know it…keep it to your self.***

If you're happy and you know
it…
Clap quietly,
Smile small,
Maybe don't post it at all.

Because joy?
It makes some people itch.
Your peace
Might just flip their switch.

They'll ask if you're glowing,
Then dim your light.
They'll scroll right past
Just out of spite.

Happiness is loud,
But envy's louder.
And not everyone claps
When you feel prouder.

You'll start soft,
"I'm just feeling good today."
And they'll twist it like
You rubbed it in their way.

So sometimes,
To protect your shine,
You learn to glow
Without a sign.
Not because joy should hide.
But because peace
Is sometimes
Best kept inside.

If you're happy and you know
it…
Keep it to yourself.
Not everyone roots
For your mental health.

***Today, you're the youngest you'd ever be.***
***Do something about it.***

You keep saying,
"Someday,"
"Later,"
"When I'm ready."
But the clock doesn't wait
For anybody.

You act like time
Is a loyal friend.
But it doesn't pause.
It just pretends.

You scroll.
You stall.
You sit in doubt.
While days
Keep moving,
In and out.

You say,
"I'll do it when I'm stronger.
Wiser.
Braver."
But what if this
Is the moment
You'll look back on
Forever?

Because the truth is,
You're not getting younger.
Not one bit.
This is the youngest
You'll ever be.

So stop waiting
For the perfect mood,
For signs,
For someone else's approval
To conclude.

Today, you're the youngest
You'll ever be.
Do something about it,
Or watch it flee.

***Before you try to figure out why someone is doing what they are, try to figure out why you're doing what you're doing.***

We all love to study people,
Decode their tone,
Unpack their reasons,
Predict the twist
Before the season.

We watch.
We analyze.
We pull it apart.
What made them leave?
What broke their heart?

We search for logic
In someone else's storm.
Draw conclusions.
Label the norm.

But rarely do we turn within
To ask ourselves,
Where have I been?
Why do I need to know so
bad?
Why does their chaos
Make me sad?
Is it empathy?
Or control in disguise?
Is it care?
Or ego in a softer size?

Why do I judge?
Why do I cling?
Why does their story
Touch my heartstring?

Because the truth is,
The things we notice
Are often echoes
Of what we carry,
What we've lived,
What we bury.

So before you decode
Someone else's scene,
Pause,
And check what yours might
mean.

***It's okay to NOT have an opinion on everything.***

Opinion.
We treat it like a badge.
Must have one.
On every trend.
Every ad, every tag.

From world peace,
To someone's shoes,
If you're breathing,
You'd better choose.

God forbid you say, "I don't know."
They'll look at you like,
"You're slow?"

So we chime in,
Fake the depth,
Rush our take
Before we've slept.

Why?
Because in our heads,
There's this loud voice:
You're in the Bigg Boss house,
You've got no choice.
Cameras on.
Judges near.
Better have a hot take,
Loud and clear.

But you're not on air.
There's no red light.
You can live in peace
Without joining the fight.

Not every silence
Needs to be filled.
Not every thought
Needs to be spilled.

It's okay to be curious,
To ask,
To wait,
To not declare
What you don't relate.

*Clarity doesn't always bring peace.*
*Sometimes, it brings decisions.*

You think that clarity
Will make things light.
That once you know,
You'll feel alright.

So you dig for answers,
Ask what's true.
You want the fog
To clear for you.

And then it does.
You see it all.
But what you feel
Isn't peace at all.

Sometimes the truth
Is hard to hold.
It asks for change.
It makes you bold.

It means you can't
Pretend anymore.
It means you might
Close a door.

It could mean leaving,
Or hearing "no."
Letting someone
You love . . . go.

It could mean starting
All over again.
Or standing up
To your oldest friend.

That's what clarity
Can sometimes do.
Not calm your heart,
But pull you through.

***You don't need more advice. You need more honesty with yourself.***

You ask around.
You take the polls.
You watch the reels.
You scroll the scrolls.

You gather thoughts.
You weigh each side.
You hope someone
Will help decide.

But deep down,
You already know.
You're not confused,
You're scared to go.

Scared to start.
Scared to end.
Scared to break.
Scared to bend.

So you dress it up
As "seeking a view."
But what you need
Is to face what's true.

It's not more wisdom
From outside walls.
It's hearing yourself
When your silence calls.

Because clarity's there.
It's just buried deep,
Under the truths
You didn't keep.

***People confuse clarity with confidence.***
***They aren't the same.***

Clarity sees,
Confidence moves.
Clarity shows,
Confidence proves.

Clarity whispers,
"This is right."
Confidence says,
"Let's stand. Let's fight."

Clarity is truth,
Confidence is trust.
Clarity is "still,"
Confidence is "must."

Clarity knows,
But doesn't shout.
Confidence acts
When there's still doubt.

Clarity is quiet,
It shows the way.
Confidence is messy,
It learns as you stray.

Clarity is found
In silent space.
Confidence builds
When you show up face to
face.

Clarity may come
Before you're ready.
Confidence wobbles
Before it's steady.

So don't confuse
The guiding light,
With the strength it takes
To face the fight.

Because one is knowing,
One is doing.
One is calm,
One is pursuing.

***Some decisions are made the moment you ask the question.***

You ask:
"Should I say yes?"
"Should I book the flight?"
"Should I text them first?"
"Should I wear white?"

It sounds like a choice,
A pause, a plan.
But the truth's already
Slipped through your hand.

Because the smile came
Before the doubt.
Your heart leaned in
Before the words came out.

You ask,
But the asking
Is just the delay.
The decision was made
On the feeling that day.

Not all choices
Are heavy or loud.
Some just bloom
Without a crowd.

You think you're unsure,
But your body knows.
Your laughter gave it
A quiet glow.

So when you ask,
"Should I go?", "Should I try?"
Notice the light
Already in your eye.

***Every end flips to a fresh start.***

What feels like a finish
May just be a space
To breathe, to grow,
To change your pace.

Not every end
Needs to sting.
Sometimes it's just
The next right thing.

So close the book,
But don't close your mind.
This isn't an ending.
It's just a sign,
To shift, to spark,
To accept the new,
And live with a lens
That flips the view.

Cut the clutter.
You've always had the knife.

Now's your time.
Welcome to
The Flip Life.

# ABOUT THE AUTHOR

Amit Dhawan is a strategist, storyteller, and culture builder, shaped by the halls of IIM Ahmedabad and sharpened by the chaos of the real world. Over the past decade, he has led award-winning agencies like Schbang Delhi, Sociowash, and Art-E, helping category-defining start-ups scale (some of which are now unicorns) and guiding legacy brands, including several Fortune 500s, through moments that demanded more than just marketing. A sought-after voice in Indian advertising, Amit is also a mentor and speaker, known for blending instinct with insight and clarity with creative depth.

Things moved fast around him. What mattered was what stayed still within. *The Flip Life* is his first book. It doesn't ask you to change your life, just the way you see it.